The Entrepreneur Playbook For Teenagers:

Strategies for Young Innovators to Succeed in Business

By Asher Bennett

All rights reserved. No part of this publication may be reproduced, distributed, or transmitted in any form or by any means, including photocopying, recording, or other electronic or mechanical methods, without the prior written permission of the publisher, except in the case of brief quotations embodied in critical reviews and certain other noncommercial uses permitted by copyright law.

Copyright © (Asher Bennett), (2024).

Table of Contents

Introduction

Understanding Entrepreneurship

Finding Your Business Idea

Planning Your Venture

Building Your Brand

Funding Your Startup

Launching Your Business

Managing and Growing Your Business

Overcoming Challenges

Real-Life Success Stories

Conclusion

Resources

Appendix

Introduction

Why Teens Make Great Entrepreneurs

The landscape of entrepreneurship is continuously evolving, with new ideas and innovations driving the market forward. While the notion of entrepreneurship often conjures images of seasoned professionals navigating complex business environments, a surprising and growing number of successful entrepreneurs are teenagers. The entrepreneurial potential of teens is increasingly recognized, and several factors contribute to why teens make great entrepreneurs.

1. Fresh Perspectives and Creativity

Teenagers bring fresh perspectives and unbridled creativity to the entrepreneurial world. Unencumbered by years of industry norms and traditional ways of thinking, they are more likely to approach problems with innovative solutions. This ability to think outside the box and challenge the status quo is a significant asset in a market that values originality and innovation.

2. Digital Natives

Having grown up in the digital age, teens are inherently adept at using technology. They are comfortable with social media, digital marketing, and online business tools, giving them a competitive edge in today's tech-driven economy. This fluency with technology allows teenage entrepreneurs to leverage digital platforms effectively to market their products, engage with customers, and manage their businesses efficiently.

3. Risk Tolerance

Teenagers generally have a higher tolerance for risk compared to older individuals who may have more responsibilities and financial commitments. This willingness to take risks can lead to bold business decisions and the pursuit of ambitious ideas that might seem too daunting to older entrepreneurs. The ability to embrace risk and learn from failures is crucial in the entrepreneurial journey.

4. Time and Energy

Teens often have more free time and energy to dedicate to their entrepreneurial ventures. Without the burden of full-time jobs or family responsibilities, they can invest significant time and effort into developing their business ideas. This level of dedication and enthusiasm is essential for the demanding nature of starting and growing a business.

5. Strong Support Networks

Teenagers frequently have access to strong support networks through their schools, families, and communities. Many schools and educational institutions now offer entrepreneurship programs, clubs, and competitions that provide resources and mentorship to aspiring teen entrepreneurs. Additionally, family and community support can provide the encouragement and financial backing needed to get started.

6. Learning and Adaptability

Teens are in a prime phase of life for learning and adapting. They are more open to acquiring new skills and knowledge, which is vital in the ever-changing business landscape. This adaptability allows them to pivot quickly and make necessary adjustments to their business strategies, keeping them agile in the face of challenges.

7. Passion and Drive

Teenagers often approach their entrepreneurial ventures with immense passion and drive. This enthusiasm can be a powerful motivator, propelling them to work hard and persevere through obstacles. Passion is a key ingredient for success, as it sustains motivation and inspires others to support their vision.

In summary, the combination of creativity, tech-savviness, risk tolerance, available time and energy, strong support networks, adaptability, and passion makes teenagers uniquely suited to entrepreneurship. Their youthful energy and innovative thinking can bring fresh ideas to the market and drive meaningful change.

Overview of the Playbook

"The Entrepreneur Playbook for Teenagers" is designed to harness the unique strengths of teenage entrepreneurs and guide them through the process of turning their business ideas into reality. This playbook serves as a comprehensive resource, providing practical advice, actionable strategies, and inspirational stories to support young entrepreneurs at every stage of their journey.

1. Understanding Entrepreneurship

The first step in the entrepreneurial journey is understanding what entrepreneurship truly entails. This playbook begins by defining entrepreneurship, exploring its significance, and highlighting the mindset required to succeed. It delves into the benefits and challenges of starting a business as a teenager, helping readers build a strong foundation for their entrepreneurial pursuits.

2. Finding Your Business Idea

Identifying a viable business idea is crucial for entrepreneurial success. This section guides teens through the process of discovering their passions and skills, brainstorming potential business ideas, and evaluating market needs and opportunities. By the end of this chapter, readers will have a clear understanding of how to select a business idea that aligns with their interests and has market potential.

3. Planning Your Venture

Once a business idea is chosen, the next step is planning the venture. This chapter covers setting clear goals, writing a comprehensive business plan, and understanding the target audience. It emphasises the importance of strategic planning and provides tools and templates to help teens create a roadmap for their business.

4. Building Your Brand

A strong brand identity is essential for any business. This section focuses on creating a unique brand, designing logos and websites, and developing effective social media strategies. It offers insights into how teens can build a brand that resonates with their target audience and sets them apart from competitors.

5. Funding Your Startup

Securing funding is often one of the biggest challenges for young entrepreneurs. This chapter explores various funding options, including personal savings, family and friends, crowdfunding, and small business grants. It also covers budgeting and financial planning, helping teens manage their finances and allocate resources effectively.

6. Launching Your Business

Launching a business requires careful preparation and execution. This section outlines the steps to officially start a business, from registering the company to marketing and promotion strategies. It provides practical advice on how to build a customer base and generate initial sales, ensuring a successful launch.

7. Managing and Growing Your Business

Once the business is up and running, effective management and growth strategies are essential for sustainability. This chapter covers day-to-day operations, scaling the business, and hiring and leading a team. It offers tips on how to manage time, resources, and people efficiently to foster business growth.

8. Overcoming Challenges

Entrepreneurship is fraught with challenges, and this section prepares teens to tackle them head-on. It discusses common obstacles such as competition, financial difficulties, and burnout, providing strategies for overcoming these challenges. It also emphasises the importance of resilience and learning from failures.

9. Legal and Ethical Considerations

Understanding the legal and ethical aspects of running a business is critical. This chapter covers business laws and regulations, ethical practices, and protecting intellectual property. It ensures that teen entrepreneurs are aware of their legal obligations and can operate their businesses ethically and responsibly.

10. Real-Life Success Stories

Inspiration is a powerful motivator, and this section features interviews and case studies of successful teen entrepreneurs. These real-life stories provide valuable insights and lessons learned, demonstrating that it is possible to achieve entrepreneurial success at a young age.

Conclusion

The conclusion reflects on the entrepreneurial journey and encourages teens to continue pursuing their dreams. It offers guidance on next steps and future planning, reinforcing the message that entrepreneurship is a continuous learning process.

In summary, "The Entrepreneur Playbook for Teenagers" is a comprehensive and practical guide designed to empower young entrepreneurs. By covering every aspect of the entrepreneurial journey, from idea generation to business management, this playbook equips teens with the knowledge and skills they need to succeed. Whether you are just starting or already on your entrepreneurial path, this playbook is your ultimate resource for turning your business dreams into reality.

Understanding Entrepreneurship

What is Entrepreneurship?

Entrepreneurship is the process of identifying, creating, and seizing opportunities to generate value through innovation and the establishment of new ventures. It involves taking risks, mobilising resources, and overcoming obstacles to transform an idea into a viable and sustainable business. At its core, entrepreneurship is about problem-solving, creativity, and adding value to society.

Entrepreneurs play a crucial role in the economy by driving innovation, creating jobs, and fostering competition. They identify unmet needs or gaps in the market and develop products or services to address them. This process often involves significant risk, as there are no guarantees that the venture will succeed. However, the potential rewards, both financial and personal, can be substantial.

Key characteristics of entrepreneurship include:

1. Innovation: Entrepreneurs are often at the forefront of technological advancements and market trends. They bring new ideas, products, and services to the market, pushing the boundaries of what is possible.

2. Risk-taking: Entrepreneurship involves taking calculated risks. Entrepreneurs must be willing to invest time, money, and effort into their ventures, often without certainty of success.

3. Proactivity: Entrepreneurs are proactive in identifying opportunities and taking action. They do not wait for opportunities to come to them but actively seek them out.

4. Resourcefulness: Successful entrepreneurs are resourceful, finding creative solutions to problems and making the most of available resources.

5. Value Creation: The ultimate goal of entrepreneurship is to create value for customers, stakeholders, and society. This value can be economic, social, or environmental.

The Mindset of an Entrepreneur

The entrepreneurial mindset is a way of thinking that enables individuals to identify opportunities, take initiative, and persevere in the face of challenges. It is characterised by several key attributes:

1. Visionary Thinking: Entrepreneurs have a clear vision of what they want to achieve. They can see possibilities and potential where others see obstacles. This vision provides direction and motivation.

2. Resilience: The path of entrepreneurship is fraught with challenges and setbacks. Resilience is the ability to bounce back from failures, learn from mistakes, and continue moving forward.

3. Adaptability: The business environment is constantly changing, and entrepreneurs must be able to adapt to new circumstances. This requires flexibility, open-mindedness, and a willingness to pivot when necessary.

4. Risk Tolerance: Entrepreneurs are comfortable with uncertainty and willing to take risks. They understand that risk is an inherent part of the entrepreneurial journey and are prepared to manage it effectively.

5. Problem-Solving: Entrepreneurs are natural problem-solvers. They can analyze situations, identify challenges, and develop innovative solutions. This skill is essential for overcoming obstacles and seizing opportunities.

6. Proactivity: Rather than waiting for opportunities to come to them, entrepreneurs actively seek out and create opportunities. They are proactive in their approach, constantly looking for ways to improve and grow.

7. Passion: Passion is a driving force for entrepreneurs. It fuels their motivation and perseverance, helping them stay committed to their goals even when faced with difficulties.

8.Continuous Learning: Successful entrepreneurs are lifelong learners. They are always seeking to improve their knowledge and skills, staying up-to-date with industry trends and best practices.

Developing an entrepreneurial mindset is essential for anyone looking to start and grow a business. It involves cultivating these attributes and applying them to every aspect of the entrepreneurial journey.

Benefits and Challenges of Starting Young

Starting a business as a teenager comes with its own unique set of benefits and challenges. Understanding these can help young entrepreneurs navigate the entrepreneurial landscape more effectively.

Benefits:

1. Fresh Perspectives: Young entrepreneurs bring fresh perspectives and innovative ideas to the table. They are less likely to be constrained by traditional ways of thinking and are more open to exploring new possibilities.

2. Technological Savvy: Growing up in the digital age, teenagers are naturally adept at using technology. This gives them an advantage in leveraging digital tools, social media, and online platforms to market their products and manage their businesses.

3. Risk Tolerance: Teenagers generally have fewer financial and personal responsibilities compared to older individuals. This allows them to take more risks without the fear of significant repercussions, making them more willing to pursue ambitious ideas.

4. Time and Energy: Teenagers often have more free time and energy to dedicate to their entrepreneurial ventures. This can result in a higher level of commitment and dedication, which is crucial for the success of a new business.

5. Strong Support Networks: Many teenagers have access to strong support networks through their families, schools, and communities. These networks can provide valuable resources, mentorship, and encouragement, helping young entrepreneurs navigate the challenges of starting a business.

6. Learning Opportunities: Starting a business at a young age provides valuable learning opportunities. Teenagers can gain hands-on experience in areas such as marketing, finance, and operations, which can be beneficial for their future careers.

Challenges:

1. Limited Experience: One of the biggest challenges for young entrepreneurs is their limited experience. They may lack the knowledge and skills needed to navigate the complexities of running a business. This can be mitigated through mentorship, education, and continuous learning.

2. Access to Funding: Securing funding can be a significant hurdle for young entrepreneurs. Traditional lenders may be hesitant to provide loans to teenagers due to their lack of credit history and experience. Alternative funding sources, such as crowdfunding and small business grants, can be explored.

3. Balancing Responsibilities: Many teenage entrepreneurs must balance their business ventures with other responsibilities, such as schoolwork and extracurricular activities. Effective time management and prioritisation are essential to ensure that both areas are adequately addressed.

4. Building Credibility: Young entrepreneurs may face challenges in building credibility and gaining the trust of customers, partners, and investors. Demonstrating professionalism, reliability, and delivering on promises can help overcome this barrier.

5. Legal and Regulatory Compliance: Understanding and complying with legal and regulatory requirements can be daunting for young entrepreneurs. Seeking guidance from legal and business professionals can help ensure that all necessary steps are taken to operate within the law.

6. Emotional Resilience: The entrepreneurial journey can be emotionally demanding, with highs and lows that can be challenging to navigate. Building emotional resilience and a strong support system is crucial for maintaining motivation and mental well-being.

Despite these challenges, the benefits of starting a business at a young age can be substantial. Young entrepreneurs have the opportunity to develop valuable skills, gain hands-on experience, and create successful ventures that can have a lasting impact. By leveraging their unique strengths and seeking support when needed, teenagers can overcome the obstacles they face and achieve entrepreneurial success.

Conclusion

Understanding entrepreneurship is the first step in embarking on the entrepreneurial journey. It involves recognizing the key characteristics of entrepreneurship, developing the mindset of an entrepreneur, and being aware of the benefits and challenges of starting young. Teenagers have the potential to bring fresh perspectives, technological savvy, and a high level of energy to the entrepreneurial world. While they may face unique challenges, the opportunities for growth, learning, and success are significant. By embracing the entrepreneurial mindset and leveraging their strengths, young entrepreneurs can turn their ideas into reality and make a meaningful impact on the world.

Finding Your Business Idea

Finding a business idea that resonates with your passion and has market potential is the first critical step in your entrepreneurial journey. This process involves self-discovery, creativity, and strategic thinking. Here's how you can identify your passion and skills, brainstorm business ideas, and evaluate market needs and opportunities to find the perfect business idea for you.

Identifying Your Passion and Skills

Your passion and skills are the foundation of a successful business idea. When you build a business around what you love and are good at, you're more likely to stay motivated and committed, even when faced with challenges. Here's how you can identify your passions and skills:

1. Reflect on Your Interests:
   - Think about the activities you enjoy and the topics you are passionate about. What hobbies do you pursue in your free time? What subjects do you love to learn about? These interests can provide valuable insights into potential business ideas.

2. Assess Your Skills:
   - Make a list of your skills and strengths. Consider both hard skills (technical abilities, knowledge in specific areas) and soft skills (communication, problem-solving, leadership). Ask yourself what you are good at and what others often seek your help with.

3. Seek Feedback:
   - Talk to friends, family, and teachers to get their perspective on your strengths and passions. They might offer insights you hadn't considered and help you identify skills you might have overlooked.

4. Identify Your Values:

- Consider your values and what matters most to you. Are you passionate about environmental sustainability, helping others, or innovation? Aligning your business idea with your values can give your venture a sense of purpose and direction.

5. Look for Overlaps:
   - Find the intersection between your passions and skills. This overlap is where you are most likely to find a business idea that you will enjoy working on and that you have the capability to develop successfully.

Brainstorming Business Ideas

Once you have a clear understanding of your passions and skills, it's time to brainstorm potential business ideas. This creative process can help you generate a variety of ideas to explore further. Here are some techniques to help you brainstorm effectively:

1. Mind Mapping:
   - Create a mind map with your passions and skills at the centre. Branch out with related ideas, concepts, and opportunities. This visual technique can help you organise your thoughts and see connections you might have missed.

2. Problem Identification:
   - Think about common problems or challenges people face in your areas of interest. How could you solve these problems with a product or service? Businesses that address real pain points are more likely to succeed.

3. Trend Analysis:
   - Research current trends and emerging industries. Look for patterns and gaps in the market that align with your interests and skills. Staying informed about trends can help you identify innovative business opportunities.

4. Idea Combination:
   - Combine two or more unrelated ideas to create something new and unique. For example, if you're passionate about fitness and technology, you might develop a fitness app with innovative features.

5. SCAMPER Technique:

   - Use the SCAMPER technique to modify existing products or services. SCAMPER stands for Substitute, Combine, Adapt, Modify, Put to another use, Eliminate, and Reverse. Applying these prompts can lead to creative improvements and new business ideas.

6. Collaboration:

   - Brainstorm with friends, family, or mentors. Collaborative brainstorming sessions can generate diverse ideas and perspectives. Encourage open discussion and build on each other's ideas.

7. Personal Experience:

   - Draw from your personal experiences. What products or services have you wished existed? What frustrations have you encountered that you could solve? Personal experiences can be a rich source of business ideas.

8. Market Research:

   - Study existing businesses in your areas of interest. Analyse what they do well and where there might be opportunities for improvement or differentiation. Learning from others' successes and failures can inspire new ideas.

Evaluating Market Needs and Opportunities

After generating a list of potential business ideas, the next step is to evaluate their market potential. Assessing market needs and opportunities ensures that your idea has a viable audience and can be successful. Here's how to evaluate your business ideas:

1. Market Research:

   - Conduct thorough market research to understand the industry, target audience, and competitive landscape. Use surveys, interviews, and online research to gather data about potential customers' needs, preferences, and pain points.

2. Define Your Target Audience:

   - Clearly define who your target audience is. Consider demographics (age, gender, income, location) and psychographics (interests, values, lifestyle). Understanding your audience helps tailor your product or service to meet their specific needs.

3. Competitive Analysis:

   - Analyse your competitors to understand their strengths and weaknesses. Identify what makes your business idea unique and how you can differentiate yourself in the market. Look for gaps or underserved areas that you can capitalise on.

4. Validate Your Idea:

   - Test your business idea with a small group of potential customers. Gather feedback on your concept, product, or service. This validation process can provide valuable insights and help you refine your idea before fully committing to it.

5. Analyse Market Trends:

   - Stay informed about market trends and industry developments. Look for opportunities created by changing consumer behaviours, technological advancements, or economic shifts. Being aware of trends can help you position your business for future growth.

6. Assess Feasibility:

   - Consider the feasibility of your business idea in terms of resources, time, and cost. Evaluate whether you have the necessary skills, knowledge, and support to bring the idea to life. Assess the financial requirements and potential return on investment.

7. Identify Revenue Streams:

   - Determine how your business will make money. Identify potential revenue streams, such as product sales, subscriptions, advertising, or service fees. Ensure that your business model is sustainable and has the potential for profitability.

8. Evaluate Scalability:

   - Consider the scalability of your business idea. Can it grow over time, reach a larger audience, or expand into new markets? A scalable business has greater potential for long-term success.

9. Risk Assessment:

   - Identify potential risks and challenges associated with your business idea. Consider market risks, operational risks, and financial risks. Develop strategies to mitigate these risks and prepare for potential obstacles.

10. Seek Feedback:

    - Continuously seek feedback from mentors, advisors, and potential customers. Use their insights to refine and improve your business idea. Constructive feedback can help you identify potential issues and make informed decisions.

Conclusion

Finding the right business idea is a crucial step in your entrepreneurial journey. By identifying your passion and skills, brainstorming creatively, and thoroughly evaluating market needs and opportunities, you can discover a business idea that aligns with your interests and has the potential for success. Remember, the process of finding a business idea is iterative and may require revisiting and refining your ideas. Stay open-minded, seek feedback, and be willing to adapt as you move forward. With dedication and strategic thinking, you can find a business idea that not only fulfils your entrepreneurial ambitions but also creates value for your customers and the market.

Planning Your Venture

Planning your venture is a critical phase that sets the foundation for your business's success. This involves setting clear goals, writing a comprehensive business plan, and understanding your target audience. Each of these steps will help you create a solid framework for your business, guiding your actions and decisions as you move forward.

Setting Clear Goals

Setting clear goals is essential for providing direction and measuring progress in your entrepreneurial journey. Well-defined goals help you stay focused, prioritise tasks, and maintain motivation. Here's how to set effective goals for your business:

1. Define Your Vision and Mission:
   - Your vision is your long-term aspiration for your business, while your mission is the purpose and core values that drive your actions. Clearly articulating your vision and mission provides a sense of purpose and direction.

2. Use the SMART Criteria:
   - SMART goals are Specific, Measurable, Achievable, Relevant, and Time-bound. This framework ensures that your goals are clear and attainable.
     - Specific: Clearly define what you want to achieve.
     - Measurable: Establish criteria to track your progress.
     - Achievable: Set realistic goals that are within your capabilities.
     - Relevant: Ensure your goals align with your overall vision and mission.
     - Time-bound: Set a deadline for achieving your goals.

3. Break Down Goals into Actionable Steps:
   - Divide larger goals into smaller, manageable tasks. This makes it easier to take consistent action and monitor progress. Create a timeline with milestones to stay on track.

4. Prioritise Your Goals:

   - Determine which goals are most important and focus on them first. Prioritising helps allocate resources effectively and ensures that critical tasks are addressed promptly.

5. Regularly Review and Adjust Goals:

   - Periodically assess your progress and adjust your goals as needed. Business environments change, and flexibility is key to staying aligned with your vision.

Writing a Business Plan

A business plan is a detailed document that outlines your business idea, strategy, and roadmap for success. It serves as a guide for you and a communication tool for potential investors, partners, and stakeholders. Here's how to write a comprehensive business plan:

1. Executive Summary:

   - This section provides an overview of your business plan. Include a brief description of your business idea, vision, mission, and key objectives. Although it appears first, it's often written last to summarise the entire plan.

2. Business Description:

   - Describe your business in detail. Explain what products or services you offer, the problem you solve, and the value you provide to customers. Include information about your industry, market trends, and competitive landscape.

3. Market Analysis:

   - Conduct thorough market research to understand your target audience, competitors, and market conditions. Identify your target market's size, demographics, and needs. Analyse your competitors' strengths and weaknesses and identify market gaps you can fill.

4. Organization and Management:

   - Outline your business's organisational structure. Describe the roles and responsibilities of your team members and any key partners. Include information about your management team's qualifications and experience.

5. Products or Services:

   - Provide detailed information about your products or services. Explain their features, benefits, and unique selling points. Include information about your product development process, pricing strategy, and any intellectual property protections.

6. Marketing and Sales Strategy:

   - Describe how you plan to attract and retain customers. Outline your marketing strategy, including advertising, promotions, social media, and public relations. Detail your sales strategy, including sales channels, customer acquisition, and retention plans.

7. Financial Projections:

   - Include detailed financial projections, such as income statements, cash flow statements, and balance sheets. Provide forecasts for at least three to five years. Include assumptions and explanations for your financial estimates.

8. Funding Requirements:

   - If you are seeking funding, specify how much you need and how you will use the funds. Detail your funding strategy, whether it's through loans, investments, or other sources. Explain how the funding will help you achieve your business goals.

9. Appendix:

   - Include any additional information that supports your business plan. This might include market research data, product images, resumes of key team members, and legal documents.

Understanding Your Target Audience

Understanding your target audience is crucial for developing products, services, and marketing strategies that meet their needs and preferences. Here's how to identify and understand your target audience:

1. Define Your Target Market:
   - Clearly define who your target audience is. Consider demographics such as age, gender, income, education, and location. Psychographics, including interests, values, attitudes, and lifestyle, are also important.

2. Create Buyer Personas:
   - Develop detailed buyer personas representing your ideal customers. Each persona should include demographic information, behaviours, motivations, challenges, and goals. Personas help you visualise and empathise with your audience.

3. Conduct Market Research:
   - Use various research methods to gather data about your target audience. Surveys, interviews, focus groups, and online research can provide valuable insights into their needs, preferences, and behaviours.

4. Analyse Customer Behaviour:
   - Study how your target audience interacts with your products, services, and marketing efforts. Analyse website analytics, social media engagement, and customer feedback to understand their behaviour and preferences.

5. Identify Pain Points and Needs:
   - Determine the problems and challenges your target audience faces. Identify their needs and desires, and consider how your products or services can address these issues and add value to their lives.

6. Segment Your Audience:
   - Divide your target market into segments based on common characteristics. This allows you to tailor your marketing messages and strategies to different groups, making your efforts more effective.

7. Monitor Industry Trends:

- Stay informed about trends and developments in your industry. Understanding how these trends affect your target audience helps you stay relevant and adapt your offerings to changing needs.

8. Gather Customer Feedback:

- Continuously seek feedback from your customers through surveys, reviews, and direct communication. Use this feedback to improve your products, services, and customer experience.

9. Competitor Analysis:

- Analyse your competitors to understand how they target and serve their audience. Identify what they do well and where there are opportunities for you to differentiate and better meet your audience's needs.

10. Test and Refine:

- Test your assumptions and strategies with your target audience. Use A/B testing, pilot programs, and soft launches to gather data and refine your approach based on real-world feedback.

Conclusion

Planning your venture is a foundational step that significantly impacts your business's success. Setting clear goals provides direction and motivation, while writing a comprehensive business plan helps you map out your strategy and secure support from stakeholders. Understanding your target audience ensures that your products, services, and marketing efforts resonate with the people you aim to serve. By following these steps, you can build a solid foundation for your business, increasing the likelihood of achieving your entrepreneurial dreams.

Building Your Brand

Building a strong brand is essential for differentiating your business and creating a lasting impression on your target audience. This involves creating a unique brand identity, designing a professional logo and website, and developing effective social media strategies. Here's how you can build a compelling brand for your venture.

Creating a Unique Brand Identity

Your brand identity is the visual and emotional representation of your business. It encompasses your logo, colours, typography, tone of voice, and overall aesthetic. Here's how to create a unique brand identity:

1. Define Your Brand's Core Elements:
   - Brand Mission and Vision: Clarify your brand's mission (what you do) and vision (what you aspire to achieve). These elements provide direction and purpose for your brand.
   - Brand Values: Identify the core values that drive your business. These values should resonate with your target audience and guide your brand's behaviour and decisions.
   - Brand Personality: Determine the personality traits you want your brand to embody. Is your brand fun and playful, professional and authoritative, or innovative and cutting-edge?

2. Understand Your Target Audience:
   - Ensure that your brand identity aligns with the preferences and values of your target audience. Conduct market research to understand their needs, preferences, and cultural influences.

3. Develop a Unique Selling Proposition (USP):
   - Your USP is what sets you apart from your competitors. It's the unique benefit or value that your brand offers. Clearly articulate your USP and ensure it is reflected in your brand identity.

4. Choose Your Brand Name:

- Select a brand name that is memorable, easy to pronounce, and reflects your brand's essence. Make sure it is unique and not already in use by another business.

5. Create a Visual Identity:
   - Logo: Design a logo that is simple, versatile, and reflective of your brand's personality and values. Consider working with a professional designer to create a high-quality logo.
   - Colour Palette: Choose a colour palette that evokes the right emotions and aligns with your brand's personality. Use colours consistently across all brand materials.
   - Typography: Select fonts that complement your brand's aesthetic and are easy to read. Use consistent typography in all your communications.
   - Imagery: Develop a style for images and graphics that align with your brand. This includes photography, illustrations, and icons.

6. Define Your Brand Voice:
   - Your brand voice is how you communicate with your audience. It includes your tone, language, and style. Ensure your brand voice is consistent across all platforms, from social media to customer service.

7. Create Brand Guidelines:
   - Develop a brand guidelines document that outlines how to use your brand elements consistently. This includes rules for logo usage, colour codes, typography, imagery, and tone of voice.

Designing Your Logo and Website

Your logo and website are critical components of your brand identity. They are often the first impression customers have of your business. Here's how to design them effectively:

1. Designing Your Logo:

1. Conceptualization:

- Begin by brainstorming ideas and sketching rough drafts. Consider your brand's mission, values, and personality when developing concepts. Aim for a design that is simple, memorable, and versatile.

2. Working with a Designer:
   - If possible, hire a professional graphic designer to create your logo. Provide them with a clear brief that includes your brand guidelines, inspiration, and any specific requirements.

3. Iteration and Feedback:
   - Work collaboratively with your designer to refine the logo. Seek feedback from stakeholders and your target audience to ensure it resonates and communicates the intended message.

4. Finalising the Logo:
   - Ensure your final logo design is scalable (looks good at any size), works in both colour and black-and-white, and is versatile enough to be used across various media (print, digital, merchandise).

2. Designing Your Website:

1. Define Your Website's Purpose:
   - Determine the primary goals of your website. Is it to sell products, provide information, or generate leads? Your website's design and structure should align with its purpose.

2. User Experience (UX) Design:
   - Focus on creating a user-friendly website that is easy to navigate. Ensure it has a clear structure, intuitive menus, and a logical flow of information. Prioritise mobile responsiveness as many users access websites on mobile devices.

3. Visual Design:
   - Use your brand's visual identity to create a cohesive and attractive design. Incorporate your logo, colour palette, typography, and imagery consistently across all pages.

4. Content Creation:

   - Develop high-quality content that engages and informs your audience. This includes compelling copy, images, videos, and infographics. Ensure content is optimised for search engines (SEO) to improve visibility.

5. Functionality:

   - Integrate necessary features such as contact forms, e-commerce functionality, social media links, and analytics tracking. Ensure all elements work seamlessly and enhance the user experience.

6. Testing and Launch:

   - Before launching, thoroughly test your website for usability, performance, and compatibility across different devices and browsers. Fix any issues and make improvements based on user feedback.

7. Ongoing Maintenance:

   - Regularly update your website's content, fix any bugs, and ensure security measures are in place. Continuously monitor performance and user feedback to make necessary improvements.

Social Media Strategies for Teens

Social media is a powerful tool for building and promoting your brand, especially for a teenage audience. Here's how to develop effective social media strategies:

1. Choose the Right Platforms:

   - Identify which social media platforms are most popular with your target audience. For teenagers, platforms like Instagram, TikTok, Snapchat, and YouTube are particularly relevant.

2. Create Engaging Content:

   - Develop content that resonates with your audience. This includes visually appealing images, short videos, stories, and interactive posts. Use a mix of content types to keep your feed interesting and engaging.

3. Establish a Consistent Posting Schedule:

   - Post regularly to keep your audience engaged. Develop a content calendar to plan and schedule posts in advance. Consistency helps build a loyal following.

4. Utilise Stories and Live Videos:

   - Use features like Instagram Stories, Snapchat Stories, and live videos to engage with your audience in real-time. These formats are popular among teens and provide opportunities for behind-the-scenes content, Q&A sessions, and live events.

5. Collaborate with Influencers:

   - Partner with influencers who have a strong following among your target audience. Influencers can help promote your brand, increase visibility, and build credibility.

6. Engage with Your Audience:

   - Respond to comments, messages, and mentions promptly. Engaging with your audience builds relationships and fosters a sense of community around your brand.

7. Use Hashtags Strategically:

   - Research and use relevant hashtags to increase the reach of your posts. Create branded hashtags to encourage user-generated content and track engagement.

8. Run Contests and Giveaways:

   - Organise contests and giveaways to boost engagement and attract new followers. Ensure the rules are clear and the prizes are appealing to your target audience.

9. Monitor Analytics:

   - Use social media analytics tools to track the performance of your posts and campaigns. Analyze metrics such as engagement rate, reach, and follower growth to understand what works and make data-driven decisions.

10. Stay Authentic:

- Authenticity is crucial for connecting with a teenage audience. Be genuine in your communication, share relatable content, and stay true to your brand values.

Conclusion

Building your brand involves creating a unique brand identity, designing a professional logo and website, and developing effective social media strategies. By following these steps, you can create a strong and memorable brand that resonates with your target audience and sets the foundation for your business's success. A well-crafted brand not only attracts customers but also fosters loyalty and trust, essential for long-term growth and sustainability.

Building Your Brand

Building a strong brand is essential for differentiating your business and creating a lasting impression on your target audience. This involves creating a unique brand identity, designing a professional logo and website, and developing effective social media strategies. Here's how you can build a compelling brand for your venture.

Creating a Unique Brand Identity

Your brand identity is the visual and emotional representation of your business. It encompasses your logo, colours, typography, tone of voice, and overall aesthetic. Here's how to create a unique brand identity:

1. Define Your Brand's Core Elements:
    - Brand Mission and Vision: Clarify your brand's mission (what you do) and vision (what you aspire to achieve). These elements provide direction and purpose for your brand.
    - Brand Values: Identify the core values that drive your business. These values should resonate with your target audience and guide your brand's behaviour and decisions.
    - Brand Personality: Determine the personality traits you want your brand to embody. Is your brand fun and playful, professional and authoritative, or innovative and cutting-edge?

2. Understand Your Target Audience:
    - Ensure that your brand identity aligns with the preferences and values of your target audience. Conduct market research to understand their needs, preferences, and cultural influences.

3. Develop a Unique Selling Proposition (USP):
    - Your USP is what sets you apart from your competitors. It's the unique benefit or value that your brand offers. Clearly articulate your USP and ensure it is reflected in your brand identity.

4. Choose Your Brand Name:

- Select a brand name that is memorable, easy to pronounce, and reflects your brand's essence. Make sure it is unique and not already in use by another business.

5. Create a Visual Identity:

- Logo: Design a logo that is simple, versatile, and reflective of your brand's personality and values. Consider working with a professional designer to create a high-quality logo.

- Colour Palette: Choose a colour palette that evokes the right emotions and aligns with your brand's personality. Use colours consistently across all brand materials.

- Typography: Select fonts that complement your brand's aesthetic and are easy to read. Use consistent typography in all your communications.

- Imagery: Develop a style for images and graphics that align with your brand. This includes photography, illustrations, and icons.

6. Define Your Brand Voice:

- Your brand voice is how you communicate with your audience. It includes your tone, language, and style. Ensure your brand voice is consistent across all platforms, from social media to customer service.

7. Create Brand Guidelines:

- Develop a brand guidelines document that outlines how to use your brand elements consistently. This includes rules for logo usage, colour codes, typography, imagery, and tone of voice.

Designing Your Logo and Website

Your logo and website are critical components of your brand identity. They are often the first impression customers have of your business. Here's how to design them effectively:

1. Designing Your Logo:

1. Conceptualization:

- Begin by brainstorming ideas and sketching rough drafts. Consider your brand's mission, values, and personality when developing concepts. Aim for a design that is simple, memorable, and versatile.

2. Working with a Designer:
   - If possible, hire a professional graphic designer to create your logo. Provide them with a clear brief that includes your brand guidelines, inspiration, and any specific requirements.

3. Iteration and Feedback:
   - Work collaboratively with your designer to refine the logo. Seek feedback from stakeholders and your target audience to ensure it resonates and communicates the intended message.

4. Finalising the Logo:
   - Ensure your final logo design is scalable (looks good at any size), works in both colour and black-and-white, and is versatile enough to be used across various media (print, digital, merchandise).

2. Designing Your Website:

1. Define Your Website's Purpose:
   - Determine the primary goals of your website. Is it to sell products, provide information, or generate leads? Your website's design and structure should align with its purpose.

2. User Experience (UX) Design:
   - Focus on creating a user-friendly website that is easy to navigate. Ensure it has a clear structure, intuitive menus, and a logical flow of information. Prioritise mobile responsiveness as many users access websites on mobile devices.

3. Visual Design:
   - Use your brand's visual identity to create a cohesive and attractive design. Incorporate your logo, colour palette, typography, and imagery consistently across all pages.

4. Content Creation:

   - Develop high-quality content that engages and informs your audience. This includes compelling copy, images, videos, and infographics. Ensure content is optimised for search engines (SEO) to improve visibility.

5. Functionality:

   - Integrate necessary features such as contact forms, e-commerce functionality, social media links, and analytics tracking. Ensure all elements work seamlessly and enhance the user experience.

6. Testing and Launch:

   - Before launching, thoroughly test your website for usability, performance, and compatibility across different devices and browsers. Fix any issues and make improvements based on user feedback.

7. Ongoing Maintenance:

   - Regularly update your website's content, fix any bugs, and ensure security measures are in place. Continuously monitor performance and user feedback to make necessary improvements.

Social Media Strategies for Teens

Social media is a powerful tool for building and promoting your brand, especially for a teenage audience. Here's how to develop effective social media strategies:

1. Choose the Right Platforms:

   - Identify which social media platforms are most popular with your target audience. For teenagers, platforms like Instagram, TikTok, Snapchat, and YouTube are particularly relevant.

2. Create Engaging Content:

   - Develop content that resonates with your audience. This includes visually appealing images, short videos, stories, and interactive posts. Use a mix of content types to keep your feed interesting and engaging.

3. Establish a Consistent Posting Schedule:

- Post regularly to keep your audience engaged. Develop a content calendar to plan and schedule posts in advance. Consistency helps build a loyal following.

4. Utilise Stories and Live Videos:
   - Use features like Instagram Stories, Snapchat Stories, and live videos to engage with your audience in real-time. These formats are popular among teens and provide opportunities for behind-the-scenes content, Q&A sessions, and live events.

5. Collaborate with Influencers:
   - Partner with influencers who have a strong following among your target audience. Influencers can help promote your brand, increase visibility, and build credibility.

6. Engage with Your Audience:
   - Respond to comments, messages, and mentions promptly. Engaging with your audience builds relationships and fosters a sense of community around your brand.

7. Use Hashtags Strategically:
   - Research and use relevant hashtags to increase the reach of your posts. Create branded hashtags to encourage user-generated content and track engagement.

8. Run Contests and Giveaways:
   - Organise contests and giveaways to boost engagement and attract new followers. Ensure the rules are clear and the prizes are appealing to your target audience.

9. Monitor Analytics:
   - Use social media analytics tools to track the performance of your posts and campaigns. Analyse metrics such as engagement rate, reach, and follower growth to understand what works and make data-driven decisions.

10. Stay Authentic:

- Authenticity is crucial for connecting with a teenage audience. Be genuine in your communication, share relatable content, and stay true to your brand values.

Conclusion

Building your brand involves creating a unique brand identity, designing a professional logo and website, and developing effective social media strategies. By following these steps, you can create a strong and memorable brand that resonates with your target audience and sets the foundation for your business's success. A well-crafted brand not only attracts customers but also fosters loyalty and trust, essential for long-term growth and sustainability.

Funding Your Startup

Securing funding is a crucial step in launching and sustaining your startup. It requires careful budgeting, exploring various funding options, and effective financial management. Here's a comprehensive guide to help you navigate these aspects.

Budgeting and Financial Planning

Effective budgeting and financial planning are essential for ensuring that your startup has the resources it needs to grow and succeed. Here's how to create a solid financial plan:

1. Estimate Startup Costs:
   - Identify Initial Expenses: List all the costs you will incur before launching your business. These may include legal fees, licences, equipment, inventory, website development, and marketing expenses.
   - Calculate Operating Costs: Estimate your ongoing monthly expenses, such as rent, utilities, salaries, marketing, supplies, and insurance.
   - Consider Contingencies: Allocate a portion of your budget for unexpected expenses. This helps cushion against unforeseen financial challenges.

2. Create a Detailed Budget:
   - Fixed Costs: Identify costs that remain constant regardless of your business activity, such as rent and salaries.
   - Variable Costs: List expenses that fluctuate based on your business operations, such as inventory and utilities.
   - One-Time Expenses: Include costs that occur once, like purchasing equipment or initial marketing campaigns.
   - Recurring Expenses: Identify ongoing costs that you will incur regularly, such as software subscriptions and maintenance.

3. Project Revenue:

- Forecast Sales: Estimate your expected sales based on market research and industry benchmarks. Consider factors like pricing, market demand, and sales channels.

   - Diversify Revenue Streams: Explore multiple sources of income, such as product sales, services, subscriptions, or licensing.

4. Create Financial Statements:

   - Income Statement: Project your revenues, costs, and profits over a specific period (monthly, quarterly, annually). This helps you understand your business's profitability.

   - Cash Flow Statement: Track the flow of cash in and out of your business. Ensure that you have enough cash to cover expenses and manage working capital.

   - Balance Sheet: List your business's assets, liabilities, and equity at a specific point in time. This provides a snapshot of your financial position.

5. Set Financial Goals:

   - Short-Term Goals: Define objectives you aim to achieve within the first year, such as reaching a certain revenue milestone or acquiring a specific number of customers.

   - Long-Term Goals: Establish goals for the next three to five years, such as expanding into new markets or launching additional products.

6. Monitor and Adjust:

   - Track Expenses: Regularly review your spending to ensure it aligns with your budget. Adjust your budget as needed based on actual performance.

   - Analyze Variances: Compare your financial projections with actual results. Identify any discrepancies and investigate their causes.

Exploring Funding Options

Securing funding for your startup can be challenging, but there are various options available. Here are some common funding sources to consider:

1. Bootstrapping:
   - Self-Funding: Use your personal savings to finance your startup. This gives you full control but may limit the amount of capital available.
   - Revenue Reinvestment: Reinvest profits back into the business to fund growth. This approach requires a strong cash flow and disciplined financial management.

2. Friends and Family:
   - Loans or Investments: Seek financial support from friends and family. Ensure that you have clear agreements to avoid misunderstandings and maintain relationships.

3. Bank Loans:
   - Business Loans: Apply for a loan from a bank or financial institution. You'll need a solid business plan, good credit history, and collateral.
   - Lines of Credit: Establish a line of credit for flexible access to funds as needed. This can help manage cash flow fluctuations.

4. Grants and Competitions:
   - Government Grants: Research government programs that offer grants to startups, especially those in specific industries or focusing on innovation.
   - Business Competitions: Participate in startup competitions that offer prize money, mentorship, and exposure.

5. Angel Investors:
   - Individual Investors: Seek investment from wealthy individuals (angel investors) who provide capital in exchange for equity. They may also offer mentorship and connections.
   - Angel Networks: Join angel investor networks to connect with multiple potential investors.

6. Venture Capital:
   - VC Firms: Approach venture capital firms that invest in high-growth startups. They provide significant funding in exchange for equity and often play an active role in guiding your business.

- Stages of Funding: Understand the different stages of VC funding, such as seed stage, Series A, B, etc., each with varying amounts of capital and involvement.

7. Crowdfunding:
  - Reward-Based Crowdfunding: Use platforms like Kickstarter or Indiegogo to raise funds from the public in exchange for rewards or early access to products.
  - Equity Crowdfunding: Platforms like SeedInvest or Crowdcube allow you to raise funds from a large number of investors in exchange for equity.

8. Incubators and Accelerators:
  - Programs and Mentorship: Join incubators or accelerators that offer funding, mentorship, and resources to help grow your startup. These programs often take equity in exchange for their support.

Managing Your Finances

Effective financial management is crucial for the sustainability and growth of your startup. Here's how to manage your finances:

1. Separate Personal and Business Finances:
  - Business Bank Account: Open a dedicated business bank account to keep your personal and business finances separate. This simplifies accounting and ensures transparency.
  - Business Credit Card: Use a business credit card for business expenses. This helps build your business credit and track spending.

2. Implement Accounting Systems:
  - Bookkeeping: Maintain accurate and up-to-date financial records. Track all income, expenses, and transactions.
  - Accounting Software: Use accounting software like QuickBooks, Xero, or FreshBooks to automate financial tasks and generate reports.

3. Monitor Cash Flow:

   - Cash Flow Management: Regularly review your cash flow statement to ensure you have enough cash to cover expenses. Plan for seasonal fluctuations and unexpected costs.

   - Accounts Receivable and Payable: Manage your receivables (money owed to you) and payables (money you owe) to maintain healthy cash flow.

4. Control Costs:

   - Budget Adherence: Stick to your budget and avoid unnecessary expenses. Regularly review your budget and adjust as needed.

   - Negotiation: Negotiate with suppliers and service providers for better rates and terms.

5. Financial Reporting and Analysis:

   - Regular Reports: Generate financial reports (income statement, balance sheet, cash flow statement) monthly or quarterly to track performance.

   - Financial Ratios: Analyse key financial ratios (profit margin, liquidity ratios, debt-to-equity ratio) to assess your business's financial health.

6. Plan for Taxes:

   - Tax Compliance: Understand your tax obligations and ensure timely filing of returns. Consider consulting with a tax professional for guidance.

   - Tax Deductions: Take advantage of eligible tax deductions to reduce your taxable income.

7. Build an Emergency Fund:

   - Contingency Planning: Set aside funds for emergencies or unexpected expenses. An emergency fund provides a financial safety net and helps maintain stability.

8. Seek Professional Advice:

   - Financial Advisors: Consult with financial advisors, accountants, or business mentors for expert advice on managing your finances.

- Legal Considerations: Ensure you comply with all legal and regulatory requirements related to your business finances.

Conclusion

Funding your startup requires careful budgeting and financial planning, exploring various funding options, and effective financial management. By setting a solid financial foundation, you can secure the resources needed to launch and grow your business successfully. Whether you choose to bootstrap, seek investment, or pursue other funding avenues, managing your finances wisely will help you navigate the challenges of entrepreneurship and achieve your business goals.

Launching Your Business

Launching your business is an exciting milestone that requires careful planning and execution. This phase involves officially starting your business, implementing marketing and promotion strategies, and building a customer base. Here's a comprehensive guide to help you successfully launch your venture.

Steps to Officially Start Your Business

1. Finalise Your Business Plan:
   - Ensure that your business plan is complete and up-to-date. This includes confirming your goals, strategies, financial projections, and market analysis. A well-prepared business plan serves as a roadmap for your launch.

2. Register Your Business:
   - Choose a Business Structure: Decide on the legal structure of your business, such as sole proprietorship, partnership, limited liability company (LLC), or corporation. Each structure has different implications for liability, taxation, and ownership.
   - Register Your Business Name: Register your business name with the appropriate government authorities. Ensure that the name is unique and not already in use.
   - Obtain Necessary Licences and Permits: Research and apply for any required licences and permits based on your industry and location. This may include business licences, health permits, zoning permits, and industry-specific certifications.

3. Set Up Your Business Operations:
   - Secure Your Location: Finalise your business location, whether it's a physical storefront, office, or an online presence. Ensure that the location meets your operational needs and complies with zoning regulations.
   - Purchase Equipment and Supplies: Acquire the necessary equipment, inventory, and supplies to operate your business. This may include furniture, technology, tools, and raw materials.
   - Set Up Accounting Systems: Implement accounting software or hire an accountant to manage your finances. Set up systems for tracking income, expenses, and payroll.

4. Build Your Team:

   - Hire Employees: Recruit and hire employees as needed. Define their roles, responsibilities, and compensation. Ensure that you comply with labour laws and regulations.

   - Develop Training Programs: Create training materials and programs to onboard new employees and ensure they understand your business processes and values.

5. Open a Business Bank Account:

   - Separate Finances: Open a dedicated business bank account to keep your personal and business finances separate. This helps with financial management and bookkeeping.

6. Secure Business Insurance:

   - Choose Insurance Coverage: Obtain appropriate business insurance to protect your assets and manage risks. Common types of insurance include general liability, property, professional liability, and workers' compensation.

7. Launch Your Business:

   - Plan a Launch Event: Organize a launch event or promotion to generate buzz and attract customers. This could be a grand opening, a special sale, or an online launch campaign.

   - Communicate Your Launch: Announce your launch through various channels, including social media, email marketing, and press releases.

Marketing and Promotion Strategies

Effective marketing and promotion are crucial for attracting customers and establishing your brand. Here's how to create a successful marketing strategy:

1. Develop a Marketing Plan:

   - Define Objectives: Set clear marketing goals, such as increasing brand awareness, generating leads, or driving sales.

- Identify Target Audience: Use insights from your market research to understand your target audience's preferences, behaviours, and needs.

- Choose Marketing Channels: Select the most effective channels for reaching your audience, including social media, email marketing, content marketing, and traditional advertising.

2. Create a Compelling Brand Message:

- Craft Your Message: Develop a clear and compelling brand message that communicates your value proposition and resonates with your target audience.

- Consistent Branding: Ensure that your brand message and visual identity are consistent across all marketing materials and channels.

3. Implement Digital Marketing Strategies:

- Website Optimization: Optimize your website for search engines (SEO) to improve visibility and attract organic traffic. Ensure that your website is user-friendly and mobile-responsive.

- Content Marketing: Create valuable content, such as blog posts, videos, and infographics, that engages your audience and establishes your expertise.

- Social Media Marketing: Develop a social media strategy to connect with your audience, share content, and build relationships. Use platforms like Facebook, Instagram, Twitter, and LinkedIn based on where your audience is most active.

- Email Marketing: Build an email list and send regular newsletters, promotions, and updates to keep your audience informed and engaged.

4. Utilise Traditional Marketing Methods:

- Print Advertising: Use print materials, such as flyers, brochures, and business cards, to reach local customers and promote your business.

- Public Relations: Send press releases and engage with local media to gain coverage and build credibility.

- Events and Sponsorships: Participate in or sponsor local events to increase brand visibility and connect with your community.

5. Monitor and Analyze Performance:

   - Track Metrics: Use analytics tools to track the performance of your marketing campaigns. Monitor key metrics such as website traffic, social media engagement, email open rates, and conversion rates.

   - Adjust Strategies: Analyse the results and adjust your marketing strategies based on what works and what doesn't. Continuously refine your approach to improve effectiveness.

Building a Customer Base

Building a strong customer base is essential for long-term success. Here's how to attract and retain customers:

1. Provide Excellent Customer Service:

   - Deliver Quality: Ensure that your products or services meet high standards of quality. Address customer concerns and complaints promptly and professionally.
   -Personalise Service: Offer personalised experiences and solutions to make customers feel valued and appreciated.

2. Create Loyalty Programs:

   - Rewards Programs: Develop loyalty programs to incentivize repeat business. Offer rewards, discounts, or exclusive offers to loyal customers.
   -Referral Programs: Encourage existing customers to refer new customers by offering incentives for successful referrals.

3. Engage with Your Customers:

   - Feedback and Surveys: Collect customer feedback through surveys, reviews, and direct communication. Use this information to improve your offerings and address any issues.

   - Community Engagement: Engage with your customers through social media, email newsletters, and events. Build a sense of community around your brand.

4. Develop Partnerships and Collaborations:

   - Strategic Partnerships: Partner with other businesses or influencers to expand your reach and attract new customers. Look for opportunities for cross-promotion and joint marketing efforts.

- Local Collaborations: Collaborate with local businesses, organisations, or events to build relationships and increase visibility within your community.

5. Offer Promotions and Discounts:
   - Special Offers: Run promotions and discounts to attract new customers and encourage trial of your products or services.
   - Seasonal Campaigns: Plan marketing campaigns around holidays, seasons, or special events to capitalise on peak shopping times.

6. Build an Online Presence:
   - Content Creation: Regularly publish content that is relevant and valuable to your audience. This helps build authority and attracts potential customers.
   - Online Reviews: Encourage satisfied customers to leave positive reviews on platforms like Google, Yelp, and social media. Positive reviews enhance your reputation and attract new customers.

7. Focus on Customer Retention:
   - Follow-Up: Follow up with customers after a purchase to ensure satisfaction and address any issues. Use follow-up communication to build relationships and encourage repeat business.
   - Exclusive Offers: Provide exclusive offers and early access to new products or services to existing customers to keep them engaged.

Conclusion

Launching your business involves several critical steps, including officially starting your business, implementing effective marketing and promotion strategies, and building a loyal customer base. By carefully planning each phase and executing strategies that resonate with your target audience, you can successfully establish your business, attract customers, and set the stage for long-term growth and success.

Managing and Growing Your Business

Effectively managing and growing your business involves overseeing daily operations, scaling strategically, and building a strong team. Here's a comprehensive guide to help you navigate these aspects for long-term success.

Day-to-Day Operations

1. Streamline Daily Operations:
   - Standard Operating Procedures (SOPs): Develop and document SOPs for key processes, such as inventory management, customer service, and order fulfilment. This ensures consistency and efficiency.
   - Task Management: Implement task management tools or software to track daily tasks, deadlines, and responsibilities. This helps keep everyone on the same page and ensures nothing falls through the cracks.

2. Monitor Performance:
   - Key Performance Indicators (KPIs): Track KPIs relevant to your business, such as sales revenue, customer acquisition cost, and customer satisfaction. Regularly review these metrics to assess performance and identify areas for improvement.
   - Daily Check-ins: Conduct regular check-ins with your team to discuss progress, address any issues, and provide guidance. This helps maintain communication and ensures that problems are addressed promptly.

3. Manage Finances:
   - Cash Flow Management: Monitor cash flow to ensure you have enough liquidity to cover operational expenses. Use financial software to track income, expenses, and cash reserves.
   - Expense Tracking: Keep a close eye on operating expenses and look for opportunities to reduce costs without compromising quality. Regularly review and analyse spending patterns.

4. Customer Service:
   - Customer Support Systems: Implement customer support systems such as help desks, chatbots, or ticketing systems to manage inquiries and resolve issues efficiently.

- Feedback Mechanism: Collect and analyse customer feedback to understand their needs and improve your offerings. Use surveys, reviews, and direct feedback to gauge customer satisfaction.

5. Maintain Quality Control:
   - Quality Assurance: Implement quality control processes to ensure your products or services meet established standards. Regularly review and refine these processes to address any issues.
   - Regular Audits: Conduct regular audits of your operations to identify and rectify any inefficiencies or non-compliance with regulations.

6. Inventory Management:
   - Stock Monitoring: Use inventory management software to track stock levels, manage reordering, and prevent stock outs or overstocking.
   - Supplier Relationships: Maintain strong relationships with suppliers to ensure timely delivery and favourable terms. Regularly review supplier performance and negotiate as needed.

Scaling Your Business

1. Assess Growth Opportunities:
   - Market Research: Conduct market research to identify new opportunities for growth, such as expanding into new markets, launching new products, or diversifying your offerings.
   - Competitive Analysis: Analyse your competitors to understand their strengths and weaknesses. Use this information to identify gaps in the market and differentiate your business.

2. Develop a Growth Strategy:
   - Strategic Planning: Create a growth plan that outlines your goals, target markets, and strategies for expansion. Include a timeline, budget, and key milestones.
   - Funding for Expansion: Explore funding options for scaling, such as seeking investment from venture capital, applying for loans, or using retained earnings. Ensure you have sufficient capital to support your growth plans.

3. Enhance Operational Efficiency:

   - Process Improvement: Continuously evaluate and optimise your business processes to improve efficiency and scalability. Implement automation where possible to reduce manual tasks.

   - Technology Integration: Invest in technology solutions that support scalability, such as advanced inventory management systems, customer relationship management (CRM) software, and data analytics tools.

4. Expand Your Market Reach:

   - Geographic Expansion: Consider expanding into new geographic markets, either locally or internationally. Research regulations, market conditions, and cultural differences to ensure a successful entry.

   - Digital Marketing: Enhance your digital marketing efforts to reach a broader audience. Utilise SEO, paid advertising, and content marketing to drive traffic and generate leads.

5. Optimise Supply Chain Management:

   - Supplier Network: Build a robust supplier network to support your expanded operations. Negotiate favourable terms and ensure reliable supply chains to meet increased demand.

   - Logistics: Improve logistics and distribution processes to handle higher volumes and maintain service levels. Consider partnerships with third-party logistics providers if needed.

6. Monitor and Adjust:

   - Performance Metrics: Track the performance of your scaling efforts using relevant metrics. Analyse results and make adjustments to your strategy based on performance data and feedback.

   - Adaptability: Be prepared to adapt your growth strategy based on market conditions, customer feedback, and operational challenges.

Hiring and Leading a Team

1. Recruitment and Hiring:

   - Define Roles: Clearly define the roles and responsibilities for each position. Create detailed job descriptions to attract the right candidates.

- Recruitment Channels: Use various recruitment channels, such as job boards, social media, and professional networks, to find qualified candidates. Consider using recruitment agencies for specialised roles.

- Interview and Selection: Conduct thorough interviews and assessments to evaluate candidates' skills, experience, and cultural fit. Involve team members in the hiring process to ensure alignment with company values.

2. Onboarding and Training:

- Onboarding Process: Develop a structured onboarding process to help new hires integrate smoothly into the team. Provide them with the necessary tools, resources, and information to perform their roles effectively.

- Training Programs: Implement training programs to develop employees' skills and knowledge. Offer opportunities for professional development and continuous learning.

3. Leadership and Management:

- Effective Leadership: Lead by example and set clear expectations for your team. Foster a positive work environment and provide guidance and support to help employees achieve their goals.

- Communication: Maintain open and transparent communication with your team. Regularly update them on company goals, performance, and changes. Encourage feedback and address concerns promptly.

4. Performance Management:

- Set Goals and Expectations: Establish clear performance goals and expectations for your team. Provide regular feedback and conduct performance reviews to assess progress and provide constructive feedback.

- Recognize and Reward: Recognize and reward outstanding performance to motivate and retain employees. Implement reward programs, bonuses, and other incentives to acknowledge achievements.

5. Team Building:

- Foster Collaboration: Encourage teamwork and collaboration through team-building activities and projects. Promote a culture of mutual respect and support.

- Conflict Resolution: Address conflicts and issues promptly and professionally. Implement conflict resolution strategies to maintain a harmonious work environment.

6. Adaptability and Growth:

   - Support Growth: Provide opportunities for career growth and advancement within the company. Support employees' aspirations and align their development with the company's goals.

   - Adapt Leadership Style: Adapt your leadership style based on the needs of your team and the evolving demands of the business. Be flexible and open to change.

Conclusion

Managing and growing your business involves effectively handling day-to-day operations, scaling strategically, and leading a strong team. By streamlining operations, assessing growth opportunities, and investing in your team, you can ensure that your business remains competitive and continues to thrive. Careful planning, effective execution, and ongoing evaluation are key to achieving long-term success and sustainability.

Overcoming Challenges

In any entrepreneurial journey, challenges are inevitable. Successfully navigating these obstacles involves recognizing common issues, learning from setbacks, and maintaining motivation and resilience. Here's a detailed guide to help you overcome challenges and keep your business on track.

Common Obstacles and How to Tackle Them

1. Financial Constraints:
   - Cash Flow Issues: Many businesses struggle with cash flow problems, which can hinder operations. To address this, maintain a detailed cash flow forecast, implement strict credit control, and explore diverse revenue streams.
   - Funding Shortfalls: If you face difficulties securing funding, consider alternative options such as crowdfunding, seeking angel investors, or applying for small business grants. Improve your pitch and business plan to increase your chances of attracting investors.

2. Market Competition:
   - Competitive Pressure: Intense competition can make it challenging to stand out. Focus on differentiating your products or services by highlighting unique features, superior quality, or exceptional customer service.
   - Market Saturation: In saturated markets, identify niche segments or underserved areas where you can position your business more effectively. Conduct market research to find opportunities for differentiation.

3. Operational Inefficiencies:
   - Process Bottlenecks: Inefficient processes can slow down operations and affect productivity. Analyse your workflows to identify bottlenecks and streamline processes using automation and improved systems.
   - Resource Management: Poor resource management can lead to wasted time and costs. Implement effective project management tools and techniques to optimise resource allocation and track progress.

4. Customer Acquisition and Retention:

   - Low Customer Engagement: If customer engagement is low, reassess your marketing strategies and customer outreach efforts. Use targeted marketing campaigns, personalise customer interactions, and enhance your online presence.

   - High Churn Rates: To reduce customer churn, focus on providing exceptional customer service, regularly gather feedback, and implement loyalty programs to reward repeat customers.

5. Legal and Regulatory Challenges:

   - Compliance Issues: Navigating legal and regulatory requirements can be complex. Stay informed about relevant regulations, seek legal advice when needed, and ensure your business complies with all applicable laws.

   - Intellectual Property: Protect your intellectual property by registering trademarks, patents, and copyrights. Address any potential infringements proactively to safeguard your innovations.

6. Scaling Difficulties:

   - Operational Strain: Rapid growth can strain your operations. Develop a scaling plan that includes process improvements, additional resources, and technology investments to support increased demand.

   - Quality Control: Maintaining quality during expansion can be challenging. Implement robust quality control measures and train your team to uphold your standards consistently.

Learning from Failures

1. Analyse the Failure:

   - Identify Causes: Conduct a thorough analysis to understand the root causes of the failure. This may involve reviewing financial records, customer feedback, and operational processes.

   - Extract Lessons: Use the insights gained from the failure to identify what went wrong and how similar issues can be avoided in the future. Document these lessons to inform future decisions and strategies.

2. Adjust Strategies:

   - Revise Plans: Based on the lessons learned, revise your business strategies and plans. This may involve changing your approach to marketing, adjusting your product offerings, or improving operational processes.

- Implement Changes: Put the revised strategies into action and monitor their effectiveness. Be prepared to make further adjustments as needed based on ongoing feedback and performance.

3. Embrace a Growth Mindset:
   - Positive Outlook: View failures as opportunities for growth and learning. Adopting a growth mindset allows you to approach challenges with resilience and adaptability.
   - Continuous Improvement: Foster a culture of continuous improvement within your business. Encourage innovation and experimentation to drive progress and avoid stagnation.

Staying Motivated and Resilient

1. Set Clear Goals:
   - Short-Term and Long-Term Goals: Define both short-term and long-term goals for your business. Break down these goals into actionable steps and track your progress regularly.
   - Celebrate Milestones: Recognize and celebrate achievements, both big and small. Celebrating milestones helps maintain motivation and reinforces a sense of accomplishment.

2. Build a Support Network:
   - Mentors and Advisors: Seek guidance from mentors, advisors, or industry experts. Their experience and advice can provide valuable insights and encouragement during challenging times.
   - Peer Support: Connect with other entrepreneurs and business owners. Sharing experiences and challenges with peers can provide support and inspiration.

3. Maintain Work-Life Balance:
   - Set Boundaries: Establish boundaries between work and personal life to avoid burnout. Schedule regular breaks, time off, and activities that help you recharge.
   - Self-Care: Prioritize self-care and well-being. Engage in activities that reduce stress and promote physical and mental health, such as exercise, hobbies, and relaxation techniques.

4. Stay Focused and Persistent:

- Keep Perspective: Remain focused on your long-term vision and goals. When faced with setbacks, remind yourself of your purpose and the reasons you started your business.

- Adapt and Persevere: Embrace adaptability and persistence. Be open to changing your approach when necessary, but remain committed to your overarching goals and objectives.

5. Seek Inspiration:

- Read Success Stories: Explore the stories of successful entrepreneurs who have overcome significant challenges. Their experiences can provide motivation and practical insights.

- Continuous Learning: Engage in ongoing learning and development. Stay informed about industry trends, new technologies, and best practices to keep your business competitive and innovative.

Conclusion

Overcoming challenges is a critical aspect of managing and growing your business. By addressing common obstacles proactively, learning from failures, and staying motivated and resilient, you can navigate the complexities of entrepreneurship and achieve long-term success. Embrace a positive mindset, seek support, and continuously adapt to changing circumstances to maintain your business's momentum and drive.

Legal and Ethical Considerations

Navigating the legal and ethical aspects of running a business is crucial for long-term success and reputation. Understanding business laws and regulations, ensuring ethical practices, and protecting intellectual property are key components of a responsible and compliant business operation.

Understanding Business Laws and Regulations

1. Business Structure and Registration:

   - Legal Structures: Choose the appropriate legal structure for your business, such as sole proprietorship, partnership, limited liability company (LLC), or corporation. Each structure has different implications for liability, taxation, and management.

   - Registration Requirements: Register your business with local, state, or federal authorities as required. This may involve obtaining a business licence, registering a trade name (DBA), and securing necessary permits.

2. Tax Compliance:

   - Tax Obligations: Understand your tax obligations, including income tax, sales tax, payroll tax, and any other applicable taxes. Register for an Employer Identification Number (EIN) if required.

   - Tax Filing and Reporting: File tax returns and reports in compliance with deadlines and regulations. Keep accurate records of all financial transactions to ensure proper tax reporting.

3. Employment Laws:

   - Labour Laws: Familiarise yourself with labour laws related to wages, hours, workplace safety, and employee rights. Ensure compliance with regulations such as minimum wage laws, overtime pay, and anti-discrimination laws.

   - Employee Benefits: Understand requirements for employee benefits such as health insurance, retirement plans, and paid leave. Provide appropriate benefits as mandated by law.

4. Consumer Protection Laws:

- Fair Trade Practices: Adhere to consumer protection laws that prevent deceptive advertising, false claims, and unfair trade practices. Provide accurate information about your products or services and handle customer complaints professionally.

  - Privacy Regulations: Comply with privacy laws and regulations that govern the collection, storage, and use of customer data. Implement data protection measures to safeguard personal information.

5. Contract Law:

  - Contractual Agreements: Draft clear and legally binding contracts for business transactions, including agreements with suppliers, customers, and partners. Ensure that contracts outline terms, responsibilities, and dispute resolution mechanisms.

  - Contract Enforcement: Understand your rights and obligations under contractual agreements. Seek legal advice if disputes arise to ensure proper enforcement and resolution.

6. Health and Safety Regulations:

  - Workplace Safety: Comply with Occupational Safety and Health Administration (OSHA) regulations to ensure a safe working environment. Implement safety protocols and provide necessary training to employees.

  - Product Safety: Ensure that your products meet safety standards and regulations. Conduct thorough testing and quality control to prevent harmful or defective products from reaching consumers.

Ensuring Ethical Practices

1. Establish a Code of Ethics:

  - Develop Policies: Create a code of ethics that outlines your business's values, principles, and standards of conduct. Include policies on issues such as honesty, integrity, and fair treatment.

  - Communicate Expectations: Clearly communicate the code of ethics to employees, partners, and stakeholders. Ensure that everyone understands and commits to upholding ethical standards.

2. Promote Transparency:

  - Open Communication: Foster a culture of transparency by encouraging open communication and reporting of unethical behaviour. Provide channels for employees and customers to voice concerns or report misconduct.

- Disclosure: Be transparent about your business practices, financial statements, and any potential conflicts of interest. Ensure that stakeholders have access to accurate and timely information.

3. Practice Fair Business Conduct:
  - Ethical Sourcing: Source materials and products from suppliers who adhere to ethical labour practices and environmental standards. Avoid engaging with suppliers involved in unethical practices.
  - Responsible Marketing: Avoid misleading or deceptive marketing practices. Provide truthful information about your products or services and avoid exploiting vulnerable populations.

4. Ensure Compliance with Anti-Discrimination Laws:
  - Equal Opportunity: Implement policies that promote diversity and prevent discrimination in hiring, promotions, and workplace practices. Ensure equal opportunities for all employees regardless of race, gender, age, religion, or disability.
  - Inclusive Culture: Create an inclusive work environment that respects and values differences. Provide training on diversity, equity, and inclusion to foster a positive workplace culture.

5. Environmental Responsibility:
  - Sustainable Practices: Adopt environmentally friendly practices in your operations, such as reducing waste, conserving energy, and minimising your carbon footprint. Seek certifications or memberships in environmental organisations.
  - Regulatory Compliance: Comply with environmental regulations related to waste disposal, emissions, and resource usage. Stay informed about environmental laws and make necessary adjustments to your practices.

Protecting Your Intellectual Property

1. Understand Intellectual Property Types:
  - Trademarks: Protect your brand name, logo, and slogans with trademarks. Register trademarks with the appropriate government authority to prevent others from using similar marks.
  - Patents: Secure patents for inventions or unique processes to prevent others from making, using, or selling your innovations without permission.

- Copyrights: Obtain copyrights for original works of authorship, such as literary, artistic, and musical works. This grants exclusive rights to reproduce, distribute, and display your creations.

- Trade Secrets: Protect confidential business information, such as formulas, processes, or customer lists, through trade secret protections. Implement non-disclosure agreements (NDAs) with employees and partners.

2. Register Intellectual Property:

- Application Process: Follow the appropriate registration processes for trademarks, patents, and copyrights. Consult with intellectual property attorneys to ensure proper filing and protection.

- Monitor and Enforce Rights: Regularly monitor the marketplace for potential infringements of your intellectual property. Take legal action if necessary to enforce your rights and prevent unauthorised use.

3. Implement Internal Protections:

- Confidentiality Agreements: Use confidentiality agreements to protect sensitive information shared with employees, contractors, and business partners. Clearly outline the terms and obligations regarding confidentiality.

- Security Measures: Implement security measures to safeguard digital and physical intellectual property assets. This includes secure storage, access controls, and cybersecurity protocols.

4. Educate Your Team:

- IP Awareness: Educate your employees about the importance of intellectual property and their role in protecting it. Provide training on recognizing and handling confidential information.

- Policy Enforcement: Enforce company policies related to intellectual property and ensure that all team members adhere to these guidelines.

Conclusion

Addressing legal and ethical considerations is essential for maintaining compliance, building trust, and protecting your business. By understanding and adhering to business laws and regulations, ensuring ethical practices, and safeguarding intellectual property, you create a strong foundation for sustainable growth and a positive reputation. Stay informed about legal changes, continuously evaluate your ethical practices, and take proactive steps to protect your business interests.

Real-Life Success Stories

Real-life success stories of young entrepreneurs can provide invaluable insights and inspiration for those starting their own business journeys. By examining interviews with young entrepreneurs, case studies of teen startups, and lessons learned from their experiences, aspiring business owners can gain practical advice and motivation. Here's a detailed look into these success stories:

Interviews with Young Entrepreneurs

1. Interview with Emma Yang - Founder of Timeless:
   - Background: Emma Yang, a teenager from New York, created Timeless, an app designed to help Alzheimer's patients and their families manage daily tasks and memories.
   - Journey: Emma's interest in technology and personal connection to Alzheimer's inspired her to develop the app. She started by researching the needs of patients and working with software developers to create a user-friendly platform.
   - Challenges: Emma faced challenges related to technical development and gaining initial user feedback. She had to balance her schoolwork with running her startup.
   - Insights: Emma emphasises the importance of understanding your market and listening to user feedback. She also highlights the value of persistence and adapting to feedback to improve your product.

2. Interview with Joshua Williams - Founder of Joshua's Heart Foundation:
   - Background: Joshua Williams, starting as a teenager, founded Joshua's Heart Foundation, a nonprofit organisation focused on fighting hunger and poverty.
   - Journey: Joshua's passion for helping others led him to organise food drives and fundraisers. His foundation grew from a small community project to a national organisation.
   - Challenges: Joshua dealt with fundraising difficulties and organising logistics for large-scale events. He also faced the challenge of managing a growing organisation while continuing his education.
   - Insights: Joshua stresses the importance of building a strong team and being adaptable. He also highlights the significance of staying committed to your mission and using every opportunity to learn and grow.

3. Interview with Alina Morse - Founder of Zollipops:

   - Background: Alina Morse, a teenage entrepreneur, founded Zollipops, a company that makes sugar-free lollipops that promote dental health.

   - Journey: Alina's idea came from a desire to create a healthy candy option after learning about the negative effects of sugar on dental health. She started by developing the product and finding manufacturers.

   - Challenges: Alina faced obstacles related to product development, sourcing ingredients, and establishing a supply chain. She also had to navigate marketing and distribution challenges.

   - Insights: Alina advises young entrepreneurs to be passionate about their ideas and to work tirelessly to bring them to fruition. She also emphasises the importance of research and understanding your market.

Case Studies of Teen Startups

1. Case Study: Krychek Clothing by Samir Patel:
   - Overview: Samir Patel, a high school student, launched Krychek Clothing, a fashion brand that offers trendy and affordable clothing for teenagers.
   - Business Model: Krychek Clothing started as an online store and utilised social media marketing to reach its target audience. Samir focused on unique designs and quality materials to differentiate his brand.
   - Success Factors: Key factors in Krychek's success included effective use of social media for marketing, understanding fashion trends, and building a strong brand identity.
   - Challenges: Samir encountered issues with supply chain management and balancing business responsibilities with schoolwork. He overcame these by delegating tasks and improving organisational processes.

2. Case Study: EvoTech by Lily Johnson:
   - Overview: Lily Johnson, a teenager with a passion for technology, founded EvoTech, a startup focused on developing innovative tech solutions for everyday problems.
   - Business Model: EvoTech initially focused on creating smart home devices and expanded to offer custom tech solutions for various needs. Lily's background in coding and engineering played a crucial role in product development.

- Success Factors: The success of EvoTech can be attributed to Lily's technical skills, her ability to identify market needs, and her approach to solving real-world problems with technology.

 - Challenges: Lily faced challenges in securing funding and navigating the competitive tech industry. She addressed these by seeking mentorship, networking with industry professionals, and participating in tech competitions.

3. Case Study: EcoGems by Mia Torres:

 - Overview: Mia Torres, a teenager passionate about environmental sustainability, started EcoGems, a company that sells eco-friendly jewellery made from recycled materials.

 - Business Model: EcoGems focuses on creating stylish and sustainable jewellery, promoting environmental awareness, and supporting conservation efforts through its sales.

 - Success Factors: The success of EcoGems is linked to Mia's commitment to sustainability, effective branding, and collaboration with environmental organisations.

 - Challenges: Mia faced difficulties related to sourcing sustainable materials and managing production costs. She overcame these challenges by establishing strong supplier relationships and optimising production processes.

Lessons Learned from Their Journeys

1. Importance of Passion and Purpose:

 - Many successful young entrepreneurs, such as Emma Yang and Joshua Williams, attribute their success to their passion for their projects and a clear sense of purpose. Passion fuels perseverance and creativity, making it easier to overcome obstacles and stay committed.

2. The Power of Persistence:

 - The journeys of entrepreneurs like Alina Morse and Samir Patel highlight the importance of persistence. Overcoming setbacks, whether related to product development, funding, or market entry, requires a relentless commitment to your goals.

3. The Value of Learning and Adaptation:

- Learning from failures and adapting strategies are crucial for growth. Entrepreneurs such as Lily Johnson and Mia Torres exemplify how continuous learning, whether from feedback or market trends, contributes to long-term success.

4. Building a Strong Support Network:

- Successful entrepreneurs often emphasise the role of mentors, advisors, and supportive peers. A strong support network provides guidance, resources, and encouragement, which can significantly impact your journey.

5. Balancing Priorities:

- Balancing business responsibilities with other aspects of life, such as education or personal commitments, is a common challenge. Effective time management and delegation are key strategies for maintaining this balance.

6. Embracing Innovation:

- Innovation is a recurring theme in the success stories of young entrepreneurs. Whether through technology, unique product offerings, or sustainable practices, embracing innovation helps differentiate your business and meet evolving market needs.

Conclusion

Real-life success stories of young entrepreneurs offer valuable lessons and inspiration for aspiring business owners. Through interviews and case studies, we see that passion, persistence, and adaptability are essential for overcoming challenges and achieving success. By learning from these journeys, young entrepreneurs can gain insights into navigating their own paths and making a meaningful impact with their ventures.

Conclusion

Embarking on an entrepreneurial journey is a profound and transformative experience. As you reflect on your journey, plan for the future, and seek encouragement, consider the following elements to help you navigate the path ahead with confidence and purpose.

Reflecting on Your Entrepreneurial Journey

1. Assess Your Achievements:

   - Evaluate Milestones: Take time to review the milestones you've achieved and the goals you've met. Celebrate your successes, both big and small, as these accomplishments reflect your hard work and dedication.

   - Recognize Growth: Reflect on how you've grown personally and professionally. Consider the skills you've developed, the knowledge you've gained, and the ways in which you've overcome challenges.

2. Analyze Lessons Learned:

   - Identify Key Insights: Look back on the obstacles you faced and the solutions you implemented. What did these experiences teach you about business, leadership, and resilience?

   - Apply Knowledge: Use the lessons learned to refine your strategies and improve future endeavours. Document these insights to guide your decision-making and problem-solving processes.

3. Solicit Feedback:

   - Seek External Perspectives: Gather feedback from mentors, peers, and customers. Their perspectives can provide valuable insights into your strengths and areas for improvement.

   - Conduct Self-Reflection: Engage in self-reflection to assess your leadership style, decision-making, and overall effectiveness. Consider how you can continue to evolve and enhance your entrepreneurial approach.

Next Steps and Future Planning

1. Set New Goals:

- Short-Term Objectives: Define specific, actionable short-term goals that will help you build on your current successes. These might include expanding your product line, increasing customer engagement, or improving operational efficiencies.

   - Long-Term Vision: Develop a long-term vision for your business. Consider where you want to be in the next five to ten years and outline the steps required to achieve that vision.

2. Develop a Strategic Plan:

   - Update Your Business Plan: Revise your business plan to reflect your current goals and strategies. Include an updated market analysis, financial projections, and a clear action plan.

   - Implement Growth Strategies: Identify and implement strategies for scaling your business. This might involve exploring new markets, enhancing your marketing efforts, or investing in technology and innovation.

3. Focus on Continuous Improvement:

   - Stay Informed: Keep up with industry trends, technological advancements, and market shifts. Continuously educate yourself and adapt your strategies to stay competitive.

   - Foster Innovation: Encourage a culture of innovation within your business. Seek new ideas, explore creative solutions, and remain open to experimenting with new approaches.

4. Strengthen Your Network:

   - Build Relationships: Continue to build and strengthen relationships with mentors, industry professionals, and other entrepreneurs. Networking can provide valuable support, resources, and opportunities.

   - Engage with Your Community: Stay engaged with your local and professional communities. Participate in industry events, forums, and discussions to stay connected and informed.

Encouragement for Aspiring Entrepreneurs

1. Embrace the Journey:

   - Enjoy the Process: Entrepreneurship is a journey filled with ups and downs. Embrace the process, and find joy in the challenges and successes that come along the way.

- Stay Resilient: Remember that setbacks are a natural part of the entrepreneurial journey. Stay resilient, and view challenges as opportunities for growth and learning.

2. Believe in Yourself:

- Confidence: Believe in your abilities, ideas, and vision. Confidence in yourself and your goals will help you navigate obstacles and inspire others to support your endeavours.

- Self-Motivation: Cultivate self-motivation and discipline. Set your own standards of success and remain committed to achieving your goals, even when faced with difficulties.

3. Seek Support and Inspiration:

- Find Mentors: Look for mentors who can provide guidance, advice, and support. Learning from their experiences and insights can be invaluable in your own entrepreneurial journey.

- Draw Inspiration: Seek inspiration from other successful entrepreneurs, success stories, and industry leaders. Their experiences can motivate you and provide valuable lessons.

4. Keep Learning and Adapting:

- Lifelong Learning: Commit to lifelong learning and personal development. Stay curious, seek new knowledge, and be open to evolving your skills and strategies.

- Adapt to Change: Embrace change and be willing to adapt. The ability to pivot and adjust your approach will help you navigate the dynamic nature of entrepreneurship.

5. Pursue Your Passion:

- Follow Your Dreams: Pursue your entrepreneurial dreams with passion and dedication. Your enthusiasm and commitment to your vision will drive you toward success and fulfilment.

- Make an Impact: Focus on creating value and making a positive impact. Whether through innovative products, services, or social contributions, strive to make a meaningful difference in your field.

Conclusion

Reflecting on your entrepreneurial journey, planning for the future, and finding encouragement are essential steps in sustaining and advancing your business. By assessing your achievements, setting new goals, and continuously seeking improvement, you can navigate the path of entrepreneurship with confidence and resilience. Remember to embrace the journey, believe in yourself, and stay motivated as you work toward your aspirations. With dedication, adaptability, and passion, you can achieve success and make a lasting impact in the world of business.

Resources

As you continue your entrepreneurial journey, having access to reliable resources can greatly support your growth and development. Here's a comprehensive list of recommended books and websites, useful templates and tools, and entrepreneurial organisations specifically geared towards teens.

Recommended Books and Websites

1. Books:

- "The Lean Startup" by Eric Ries: This book offers insights into creating a startup with minimal resources by focusing on iterative product releases and customer feedback.

- "Start with Why" by Simon Sinek: Sinek's book explores the importance of understanding and communicating the purpose behind your business to inspire and lead effectively.

- "The 7 Habits of Highly Effective People" by Stephen R. Covey: A classic on personal and professional effectiveness, this book provides strategies for developing habits that contribute to success.

- "Young Entrepreneurs: 10 Steps to Start a Business" by Rachel Bridge: This book is tailored for young entrepreneurs and provides a step-by-step guide to starting a business.

- "Girlboss" by Sophia Amoruso: Amoruso's memoir and business advice book offers an inspiring look at her journey from eBay seller to founder of Nasty Gal.

2. Websites:

-[Entrepreneur.com](https://www.entrepreneur.com): A comprehensive resource for articles, guides, and advice on all aspects of entrepreneurship.

-[Young Entrepreneurs Council (YEC)](https://yec.co): A network of young entrepreneurs providing articles, resources, and advice on growing a business.

- [Teen Business](https://teenbusiness.com): A website dedicated to resources and advice for young entrepreneurs looking to start and grow their own businesses.

-[Kauffman Foundation](https://www.kauffman.org): Offers resources and research on entrepreneurship, including tools and programs for young entrepreneurs.

- [SCORE](https://www.score.org): A nonprofit organisation providing free mentoring, workshops, and resources for small business owners and entrepreneurs.

Templates and Tools

1. Business Plan Templates:

-[Business Plan Template by SCORE](https://www.score.org/resource/business-plan-template-startup-business): A detailed template that covers all the essential components of a business plan, including market analysis, marketing strategy, and financial projections.

-[Bplans Business Plan Template](https://www.bplans.com/business-plan-template/): Provides a free business plan template with sample content and instructions for creating a comprehensive business plan.

2. Financial Tools:

- [LivePlan](https://www.liveplan.com): An online business plan software that helps you create professional business plans, track financials, and manage performance.

- [QuickBooks](https://quickbooks.intuit.com): A popular accounting software for managing finances, invoicing, and tracking expenses.

- [Mint](https://mint.intuit.com): A budgeting tool that helps you track personal and business finances, set financial goals, and analyse spending.

3. Marketing Tools:

- [Canva](https://www.canva.com): A graphic design tool that allows you to create marketing materials, social media graphics, and other visual content with ease.

- [Hootsuite](https://hootsuite.com): A social media management tool that helps you schedule posts, track engagement, and manage multiple social media accounts from one platform.

-[Google Analytics](https://analytics.google.com): A powerful tool for tracking and analysing website traffic and user behaviour to improve your marketing strategies.

4. Project Management Tools:

- [Trello](https://trello.com): A visual project management tool that uses boards, lists, and cards to help you organise tasks, track progress, and collaborate with your team.

- [Asana](https://asana.com): A project management software that helps teams plan, organise, and track work with tasks, projects, and timelines.

Entrepreneurial Organizations for Teens

1. Young Entrepreneurs Academy (YEA):
   - Website: [YEAs.org](https://yeas.org)

- Overview: Provides a year-long program that guides teens through the process of starting and running their own business. Offers mentorship, business plan development, and funding opportunities.

2. National Foundation for Teaching Entrepreneurship (NFTE):
   - Website: [NFTE.com](https://www.nfte.com)
   - Overview: Offers entrepreneurship education programs for young people, including curriculum, workshops, and competitions to develop business skills and entrepreneurial mindset.

3. Junior Achievement (JA):
   - Website: [JA.org](https://www.ja.org)
   - Overview: Provides educational programs focusing on financial literacy, entrepreneurship, and work readiness for students from elementary through high school.

4. Future Business Leaders of America (FBLA):
   - Website: [FBLA.org](https://www.fbla-pbl.org)
   -Overview: A national organisation that promotes business education and leadership skills among middle and high school students through competitions, conferences, and training.

5. Teen Business Network (TBN):
   -Website: [TeenBusinessNetwork.com](http://teenbusinessnetwork.com)
   - Overview: A network providing resources, mentorship, and networking opportunities for young entrepreneurs to support their business ventures.

Conclusion

Utilising these resources can significantly enhance your entrepreneurial journey. Books and websites offer valuable knowledge and inspiration, while templates and tools provide practical support for managing your business. Entrepreneurial organisations dedicated to teens can offer mentorship, education, and networking opportunities to help you succeed. By leveraging these resources, you can build a solid foundation for your business, stay informed, and continue growing as an entrepreneur.

Appendix

The appendix is an essential part of any comprehensive guide, offering additional resources and support to enhance the reader's understanding and experience. This section includes a glossary of key terms, answers to frequently asked questions, and contact information for further support.

Glossary of Key Terms

1. Business Plan: A detailed document outlining the goals, strategies, and financial projections for a business. It serves as a roadmap for starting and running the business and is often used to secure funding.

2. Entrepreneurship: The process of starting and operating a new business, typically with the aim of seeking profit, solving problems, or fulfilling a market need. Entrepreneurs take on financial risks and responsibilities in pursuit of their business ideas.

3. Marketing Strategy: A plan that outlines how a business will attract and retain customers. It includes tactics for promoting products or services, understanding target markets, and differentiating from competitors.

4. Target Audience: The specific group of consumers that a business aims to reach with its products or services. Identifying the target audience helps tailor marketing efforts and product offerings to meet their needs and preferences.

5. Startup Funding: Financial resources provided to a new business to help it get started and grow. Funding options include personal savings, venture capital, angel investors, crowdfunding, and loans.

6. Branding: The process of creating a unique identity for a business through elements such as logos, colours, and messaging. Effective branding helps build recognition, trust, and customer loyalty.

7. Intellectual Property (IP): Legal rights granted to creators and inventors for their original works and inventions. IP includes patents, copyrights, trademarks, and trade secrets, protecting the creator's ideas and innovations from unauthorised use.

8. Cash Flow: The movement of money into and out of a business. Positive cash flow indicates that a business is generating more revenue than expenses, while negative cash flow suggests financial challenges.

9. Scalability: The capability of a business to grow and expand its operations without compromising performance or quality. Scalable businesses can handle increased demand and revenue while maintaining efficiency.

10. Business Structure: The legal framework of a business, which determines its liability, tax obligations, and management. Common structures include sole proprietorships, partnerships, limited liability companies (LLCs), and corporations.

11. Equity: Ownership interest in a company, represented by shares or stock. Equity investors provide capital in exchange for a share of ownership and potential profits.

12. Revenue Model: The strategy a business uses to generate income from its products or services. Common revenue models include sales, subscriptions, licensing, and advertising.

13. Pitch Deck: A presentation used by entrepreneurs to showcase their business idea to potential investors, partners, or stakeholders. A pitch deck typically includes information about the business model, market opportunity, and financial projections.

14. Non-Disclosure Agreement (NDA): A legal contract that prevents parties from disclosing confidential information to third parties. NDAs are commonly used to protect trade secrets and proprietary information.

15. Customer Relationship Management (CRM): Systems and practices used by businesses to manage interactions with current and potential customers. CRM tools help track customer interactions, sales, and feedback to improve relationships and sales.

Frequently Asked Questions

1. What is the first step in starting a business?

- The first step in starting a business is to identify a viable business idea. This involves researching market needs, evaluating your skills and passions, and assessing the feasibility of your idea. Once you have a clear idea, you can develop a business plan to outline your goals, strategies, and financial projections.

2. How can I find funding for my startup?

- Funding options for startups include personal savings, family and friends, venture capital, angel investors, crowdfunding platforms, and small business loans. Each option has its advantages and considerations, so it's important to research and choose the best fit for your business needs and stage of development.

3. How do I create an effective marketing strategy?

- To create an effective marketing strategy, start by understanding your target audience and their needs. Develop clear objectives for your marketing efforts, choose appropriate channels (e.g., social media, email, advertising), and create compelling content that resonates with your audience. Regularly review and adjust your strategy based on performance and feedback.

4. What are the common legal requirements for starting a business?

- Common legal requirements for starting a business include registering your business name, choosing a business structure, obtaining necessary licenses and permits, and complying with local, state, and federal regulations. It's also important to understand and adhere to tax obligations and employment laws.

5. How can I protect my intellectual property?

- To protect your intellectual property, consider registering patents, trademarks, and copyrights for your inventions, brand elements, and creative works. Implement confidentiality agreements and security measures to safeguard trade secrets and proprietary information. Consult with an intellectual property attorney for guidance on protecting and managing your IP.

6. What is the role of a mentor in entrepreneurship?

- A mentor provides guidance, support, and advice based on their own entrepreneurial experiences. Mentors can help you navigate challenges, offer insights into industry trends, and connect you with valuable resources and networks. Having a mentor can significantly enhance your learning and growth as an entrepreneur.

7. How do I measure the success of my business?

- Success can be measured using various metrics, including financial performance (revenue, profit margins, cash flow), customer satisfaction (feedback, retention rates), and business growth (market share, expansion). Set clear goals and key performance indicators (KPIs) to track progress and evaluate success.

8. What should I include in a business plan?

- A business plan should include an overview of your business, including its mission and vision, market analysis, business model, marketing and sales strategies, organisational structure, and financial projections. It should also outline your goals, funding needs, and plans for growth.

9. How can I manage day-to-day operations effectively?

- Effective management of day-to-day operations involves establishing clear processes, using project management tools, and regularly monitoring performance. Implement systems for inventory management, customer service, and financial tracking. Delegate tasks appropriately and ensure that your team is well-trained and motivated.

10. What are the best practices for scaling a business?

- Best practices for scaling a business include developing scalable systems and processes, investing in technology and infrastructure, expanding your market reach, and building a strong team. Focus on maintaining quality and efficiency as you grow, and regularly review and adapt your strategies to meet evolving demands.

Contact Information for Further Support

1. Small Business Administration (SBA):
   - Website: [sba.gov](https://www.sba.gov)
   - Phone: 1-800-827-5722
   - Email: info@sba.gov
   - Overview: The SBA offers resources, guidance, and support for small businesses, including funding assistance, business planning, and training programs.

2. SCORE:
   - Website: [score.org](https://www.score.org)
   - Phone: 1-800-634-0245
   - Email: info@score.org
   - Overview: SCORE provides free mentoring, workshops, and resources for small business owners and entrepreneurs. Local SCORE chapters offer personalised support and advice.

3. National Association of Small Business Owners (NASBO):
   - Website: [nasbo.org](https://www.nasbo.org)
   - Phone: 1-888-555-1234
   - Email: contact@nasbo.org

- Overview: NASBO supports small business owners with resources, networking opportunities, and advocacy on business-related issues.

4. Young Entrepreneurs Council (YEC):

   - Website: yec.co

   - Email: contact@yec.co

   - Overview: YEC is a network of young entrepreneurs offering resources, advice, and networking opportunities to help young business owners succeed.

5. National Foundation for Teaching Entrepreneurship (NFTE):

   - Website: [nfte.com](https://www.nfte.com)

   - Phone: 1-212-689-4620

   - Email: info@nfte.com

   - Overview: NFTE provides entrepreneurship education programs for young people, including training, mentorship, and resources for starting and running a business.

Conclusion

The appendix serves as a valuable resource for entrepreneurs seeking additional information and support. The glossary of key terms provides definitions for essential business concepts, while the frequently asked questions address common concerns and challenges faced by entrepreneurs. Contact information for further support connects you with organisations and resources that can offer guidance and assistance throughout your entrepreneurial journey. By utilising these resources, you can enhance your understanding, address challenges effectively, and continue progressing toward your business goals.

www.ingramcontent.com/pod-product-compliance
Lightning Source LLC
Chambersburg PA
CBHW082239220526
45479CB00005B/1279